PRAYING WITH CHILDREN

PRAYING WITH CHILDREN

28 Prayer Services for Various Occasions

GWEN COSTELLO

ILLUSTRATIONS by Bette Schlosser

XXIII

TWENTY-THIRD PUBLICATIONS

Mystic, Connecticut

Second printing 1990

Twenty-Third Publications
185 Willow Street
P.O. Box 180
Mystic, CT 06355
(203) 536-2611

ISBN 0-89622-439-2
Library of Congress Catalog Card Number 90-70560

CONTENTS

INTRODUCTION

Dear DREs and principals, catechists and teachers, parents and parish leaders, and all who gather with children on a regular basis:

All of us have occasion to be with groups of children. Whether we do so daily, weekly, or monthly, we can use these times to teach children to pray. Knowing how busy we all are, and also knowing how difficult it sometimes is to find the proper words to say or appropriate actions to do, I have written this book. It is intended to introduce children to the wonder and delight of group prayer.

I hope that these services will demonstrate that prayer times needn't be long and drawn out. Meaningful prayer experiences can be brief and simple, as indeed they *should be* for children.

It's Always Appropriate to Pray

Prayer can be based on every conceivable childhood experience: happy times, sad times, birthdays, church feasts, national holidays, new beginnings, and fond farewells. And, prayer times can center on what's happening "here and now" within any particular group.

For example, if the children in a group are often fighting and quarreling, it's time for prayer. If they have worked toward and achieved a longed-for goal, it's time for prayer. If everyone in the group is feeling blah in January, or excited by the coming of spring in April, it's time for prayer.

My fondest hope is that catechists, teachers, and other adults will begin, after using some of these services, to develop their own group prayers. They can start by addressing a particular need the children in their group have. Are they constantly noisy and disruptive? What about a prayer service that focuses on being quiet and at peace?

Are the children worried about something or someone in particular? What about a service that assures them of God's love and care?

Has something wonderful happened in their town, school, or parish? What about a prayer service to say thanks to God? There are as many possibilities for prayer as there are life experiences.

I hope, too, that the adult leaders who use these services will invite children to help prepare them. Given the opportunity and the motivation, children can come up with reasons for prayer that never occur to adults. They can think of items or symbols for their prayer table, and make drawings or posters to illustrate themes. And, once introduced to the process, they can also choose their own scripture readings.

Children should be invited to take turns leading the services, and they should be involved as leaders or readers whenever possible. Ritual actions or activities should always be included in prayer services, so that *every* child has an opportunity to respond and participate. The more involved children become, the more the prayer experience is "theirs."

The more we pray with children the better, and the more we pray with them, the sooner they will become persons of prayer—on their own.

How These Services Can Be Used

The 28 services in this book are intended to be used by teachers, catechists, and other adults, from September through May or June. They cover the seasons of the year and the liturgical seasons and feasts, but they also celebrate many other expected and unexpected happenings in the lives of children. For example, there are two services each for Thanksgiving, Advent, Christmas, Lent, Easter, and Pentecost. But there is also a service for birthdays, one for welcoming new children, one for the death of a pet, and one for helping children make wise choices in difficult circumstances.

At the end of the book there is a Theme Index. Under each theme is listed all the services that relate to it in any way. Any given service might appear several times within this index, since indeed, many of the services are related to more than one topic. For example, "Time to Say I'm Sorry" appears under "Sacraments" as well as under "Liturgical Seasons." And, "We Learn from Mary" appears under "Christmas" as well as under "Mary and the Saints."

Also at the back of the book is an Appendix. This section contains all of the prayers and prayer refrains that appear in these services. These prayers are listed together for convenience, in case adult leaders want to review them, or in case they want the children to practice or memorize them before a service.

Who Should Use These Services?

All who gather with children on a regular basis can use these services. They can be used as part of a meeting, a class, a sacrament practice session, a family meal. They can also be used with parent groups who gather to discuss ways to grow in faith and prayer with their children. They can be done in church, in classrooms, in meeting rooms, and in homes. In some cases, slight adaptations will have to be made to adjust to the environment. For example, if a given service is done in a home, the "prayer table" might actually be a dining room or kitchen table.

"As written" these services will probably work best with children in grades two through six. (I am presuming that at least some of the children will be able to serve as Readers.) However, many of the services, if not all, can be adapted for younger and also older groups of children. I have used them successfully with seventh and eighth graders and even with preschoolers (in this case by using only certain sections of any given service and by doing the Readings myself).

When possible and appropriate, I have used words or phrases from the Mass and the Bible in these services. I hope that this will help children make "connections" between liturgy, the Bible, and life, and to become familiar enough with biblical and liturgical words and phrases to use them often in their prayer.

One final note: Permission is granted to duplicate these services for the children in classes or groups who participate in them.

A BLESSING FROM JESUS

Note: This service should be prayed during your first class or meeting of the year. However, since it focuses as much on prayer as on welcoming, you might adapt it for use throughout the year simply by omitting the opening paragraph.

To Prepare: Set up in your prayer space a Bible (open to Matthew 19: 13-15), and a candle.

LEADER: Welcome, children, welcome! Today we are beginning a journey of faith together. On this journey we will often meet Jesus, and we will talk to him and listen to him. This talking and listening is what we call prayer. Every time we gather for class, we will spend some of our time at prayer. But how do we know that Jesus wants us to spend time with him? He tells us so in God's Word, the Bible. Let's listen now to what he says.

READER: A reading from the Gospel of Matthew:

Some people brought children to Jesus
for him to place his hands on them
and to pray for them,
but the disciples scolded the people.
Jesus said to the disciples,
"Let these children come to me
and do not stop them,
because the kingdom of heaven
belongs to such as these."
Then Jesus placed his hands
on the children and blessed them.

This is the Word of the Lord.

ALL: Thanks be to God.

LEADER: (As you lead the following brief imaginary prayer, speak softly and slowly.)

Children, close your eyes now and make believe that you are one of the children in the story we just heard.
  Picture the grown-ups trying to push you away. How do you feel? Imagine now that Jesus is speaking to you: "Come here," he says, "don't be afraid." He places one hand on your shoulder and another on your head. How do you feel now?
  You realize that this is your chance to say something to Jesus. He smiles at you and you know that you can tell him whatever you want. Talk to him now in your own words. (Pause for a longer time.)

LEADER: Now open your eyes and take the hand of the person next to you. Together let us praise and thank Jesus.

Thank you for your blessing, Jesus.

ALL: Thank you for your blessing, Jesus.

LEADER: Thank you for your love for me.

ALL: Thank you for your love for me.

LEADER: Please bless me every day.

ALL: Please bless me every day.

LEADER: Amen. Alleluia. Amen.

ALL: Amen. Alleluia. Amen.

Welcoming New Children
GOD KNOWS US BY NAME

Note: This service can be used to welcome a child who enters the group as a stranger, or, it can be adapted for use at the beginning of the school year to help an entire class of children get acquainted.

To Prepare: Place in your prayer space a Bible (open to 1 Kings 8:41-43), small blank pieces of paper (4" x 4"), and pencils or markers for each child.

LEADER: Dear God, you are our creator and our parent. You know each of us by name.

SIDE ONE: We are boys and we are girls, and you know each of us by name.

SIDE TWO: Some of us have lived here a long time, and some of us are new, but you know all of us by name.

LEADER: We are all your children. Gather us in your arms and teach us how to welcome one another as you welcome us.

READER: A reading from the Book of Kings:

We welcome any of you
who are strangers
from distant places.
We welcome you in God's name.
When we pray together,
we will hear about God;
we will learn about God's
mighty hand and outstretched arm.
And when we pray together as one,
God will hear all our prayers.

It is God's wish that all the peoples of the earth know the name of God and revere it.

This is the Word of the Lord.

ALL: Thanks be to God.

LEADER: In this reading from God's Word, King Solomon invited strangers to worship with the Israelite people.

Because God's Word is meant for us, too, this reading tells us that we are all invited to rest in God's arms. God knows all of us and loves all of us—even though we don't yet know one another well. Let us now welcome _____ (name of new child), who is new to our class (or group) by offering him/her a sign of peace.

(Each child should say to the new child:)
"Peace be with you. My name is _____."

(When all have greeted the new child in this way, distribute the papers and pencils [or markers]. Invite children to make cards for the new member on which they write or draw something about themselves. The new child should also do a card about himself (herself).

When these are finished, invite children to share what they have written or drawn with the entire group. After the explanations, invite children to give their cards to the new member. His (her) card can be given to the whole group, and be put in a place of honor. Then continue with the following closing prayer:)

LEADER: God, our creator and our parent, thank you for calling each of us by name. Thank you for letting us get to know _____ (new child's name). May all of us grow together in love for you and for one another. We ask you this in the name of Jesus Christ, your son, our Lord...

ALL: Amen.

(If all the children are new to one another, first spend some time getting acquainted as a group, and then have a group greeting of peace and a group sharing of cards.)

EACH OF US IS SPECIAL

Note: This service might most appropriately be used in the Fall when leaves are changing color and children are very conscious of them.

However, it can certainly be used at any time of the year, especially when you want to focus on the unique gifts of each child.

To Prepare: Arrange chairs in a semi-circle, facing a table on which is placed a Bible (open to 1 Corinthians 12: 12-26), a roll of tape, and a large piece of posterboard (on which a tree trunk and bare tree limbs are pre-drawn). Write at the bottom of the posterboard: "We all belong to Christ."

As the children enter the room, hand each a piece of colored construction paper and a pencil. Ask them to draw a leaf, any kind they wish. (Very young children might have to trace from a pattern.) Each child should print or write his or her name on the leaf and then cut it out. When all the leaves are ready, ask the children to hold them as you begin the service.

LEADER: May the peace of Jesus Christ be with you.

ALL: And also with you.

LEADER: We gather today to listen to the Word of God, to think about its meaning, and to respond to it. In other words, we have come together to pray. We do this as a group, but we are not just any group. We are Christian people brought together by our faith in Jesus Christ.

Each of us is unique and each of us is special. Each of us has been given the gift of faith and with that gift we can help and support one another. This is how Saint Paul describes us:

READER ONE: A reading from Paul's first letter

to the Christians at Corinth:

We each have only one body,
but our bodies have many parts.
And all of the parts are important.
My eyes cannot say to my hands:
I am more important, so I don't need you.
And my head can't say to my feet:
I do all the thinking, so I don't need you.

READER TWO: Even those parts of my body
that don't seem important
are essential for my well being.
Now this is the point:
We Christians are the body of Christ.
Every one of us is a member of it.
Christ is the head, and we are the parts;
all of us are important,
and all of us need one another.

This is the Word of the Lord.

ALL: Thanks be to God.

LEADER: Another symbol we can use to show our specialness as a group is a tree. As we know, especially at this time of the year, a tree has many leaves, and each leaf is special and unique, even when it falls to the ground.

As a sign that we are a special group, brought together by our faith in Jesus, let us now place our leaves on this tree, which we will keep in a place of honor in our class. Please come forward one by one, with your leaves.

(Take each leaf and attach it to the tree with tape while saying: "_____, you are a member of the Body of Christ."

THANK YOU, GOD, FOR PETS

Note: This service can be used on the feast of Saint Francis of Assisi, or at any time of the year for a "blessing of pets." If children are not able to bring live pets, you might have them draw a picture of the pet they want to thank God for. Another alternative would be to have them print the names of their pets on large pieces of paper, which they can place on the prayer table at the appointed time.

To Prepare: With the children helping, cut pictures of pets from old magazines and paste these on a poster. Beneath the pictures, print: "Thank you, God, for pets." Prior to the service, place this poster in a visible place.

LEADER: All creatures great and small, praise and bless the Lord.

ALL: All creatures great and small, praise and bless the Lord.

READER ONE: We give you thanks, God of all creation, for your gifts…
- for the gifts of sun, moon, and stars
- for the wind and the water
- for the clouds in the sky
- for the gift of rain that waters the earth
- for birds and fish, and all the creatures of the sea and sky
- for wild animals and tame animals
- And especially for our pets who love us, play with us, and watch over us.

LEADER: We give you thanks,

God of all creation, for your gifts.

ALL: We give you thanks,
God of all creation, for your gifts.

READER TWO: Our pets can make us laugh
because of the silly things they do.
They can cheer us up when we feel sad,
especially when they are happy to see us.
Sometimes we have to work hard
to take care of our pets,
because they can't take care of themselves.
Sometimes we even get angry with them
because they are so messy,
or they get into the wrong things.
But even when we get mad at them,
our pets still love us—no matter what.

LEADER: We ask you, God of all creation, to help us take
good care of our pets. Thank you for the happiness they give us.

(Now invite participants to come forward with
their pets [or pictures, or names of pets]. As each
presents his or her pet [or drawing or name], say:
Thank you, God, for [name of pet]. Place the
drawings and or names on the prayer table.
When all pets have been named, conclude with
the final blessing.)

LEADER: All creatures great and small,
praise and bless the Lord. Amen.

ALL: All creatures great and small,
praise and bless the Lord. Amen.

Honoring God's Holy Ones
THE SAINTS PRAISED GOD

Note: This service can be used on or near the feast of All Saints (November 1). It reminds children that saints are people who trust in God and that they, too, can be like the saints.

To Prepare: In your prayer space, place a Bible (open to Psalm 126), a candle, and, if available, a picture or pictures of saints, and a book or books about saints.

LEADER: The grace of our Lord Jesus Christ and the love of God and the fellowship of the Holy Spirit be with you all.

ALL: And also with you.

LEADER: We celebrate national holidays to honor the heroes and heroines of our country, and we also have special days to honor those who fought and died in our wars.

READER ONE: We celebrate the feast of All Saints
for a similar reason,
but the people we honor were heroic
not because of great deeds they did,
but because they lived good lives.
Mostly they lived and died
for God and others.
They put their energy, their intelligence,
their talent, and often their material goods
at the disposal of God and other people.

READER TWO: Even when life was very hard for them,
when there was sickness, or poverty,
or suffering of any kind in their lives,
the saints praised God.

READER THREE: Psalm 126 says:

Those who sow in tears,
shall reap with shouts of joy.
This means that even though
there is sadness in life,
when we count on God,
we will again rejoice.

READER FOUR: Saints are people who have learned to say:
God has done great things for us;
we are glad indeed.
Although we go forth weeping,
carrying the seed to be sown,
we shall come back rejoicing,
carrying our sheaves.

LEADER: Let us now pray to the saints, asking them for the
kind of courage they had, that we, too, might live
our lives for God and others.

(Before you begin, give the children a moment to
think of the saint they will pray to. Their name
saints would be an obvious choice, but some may
not have been named for a saint. Give a few
suggestions, so that each child has a saint to pray
to. Begin this litany yourself and continue until
every child has had a turn.)

LEADER: Saint Peter...

ALL: Pray for us.

LEADER: Saint Lucy...

ALL: Pray for us.

LEADER: Saint Maria Goretti...

ALL: Pray for us.

LEADER: (When all have prayed:)

All you saints of heaven, teach us to live for God and others. Speak to God for us that we might have the kind of courage you showed in your lives. We ask this in the name of the Father, and of the Son, and of the Holy Spirit.

ALL: Amen.

(If you have pictures or books displayed on your prayer table, invite children to now spend some time looking at and discussing these.)

WE SAY THANKS TO GOD

Note: This service is obviously in preparation for Thanksgiving, though it can certainly be adapted for general use. Before you begin, invite children to write out on a slip of paper something for which they are particularly grateful. They should hold on to these slips until they are called for during the service.

To Prepare: Place in your prayer space a Bible (open to Psalm 111), a bowl, and any other items that symbolize thanksgiving for you.

READER ONE: Jesus, we have come to you once again
for your blessing.
We have come to talk to you and to listen.
Teach us how to pray.

LEADER: Every day is a good day for saying thanks to God. And it is especially good to say our thanks—together—as we prepare for our national feast of Thanksgiving.
   But how should we do this? Actually, we can say thank you to God in many different ways—as part of our morning or evening prayers, as part of our meal prayers, or during our class prayers. And we can also say thank you in small, quiet ways all through the day.

READER TWO: When we do well at a hard task in school,
we can pray: Thank you, God,
for the chance to grow and learn.

READER THREE: When we play in the
autumn leaves after school,
we can whisper:
Thank you, God, for friends and fun.

READER FOUR: When we gather in the evening

with our parents and family,
we can say in our hearts:
Thank you, God, for people who love us.

LEADER: We can also pray our thanks by using prayers
from God's Word, the Bible. Let us now listen to
this prayer from Psalm 111:

READER ONE: With all my heart, I thank God.
How wonderful are the things God does.
God provides food for us,
and never forgets to watch over us.
Holy and mighty is our God.
How wise are we when we
proclaim God's goodness
in words of thanks and praise.

This is the Word of the Lord.

ALL: Thanks be to God.

LEADER: I now invite you to come forward, one by one,
with the slips of paper you have prepared. As
you place them in the bowl, say aloud, "Thank
you, God." The rest of us will answer "Amen."

(When all have placed their slips in the bowl,
pray the closing prayer.)

LEADER: (holding the bowl high:) We proclaim your
goodness, our God. Let this bowl be a sign of our
thanks to you. Let it remind us to say "thank
you" often to you and to others. We ask this in
the Name of Jesus Christ, our Lord.

ALL: Amen.

(Decide together where to display the bowl.)

Remembering Her Great Faith

WE LEARN FROM MARY

Note: Use this service throughout the four weeks of Advent. You might want to combine it with the blessing of and prayers around your class Advent wreath.

To Prepare: Place in your prayer space a Bible (open to Luke 1: 39-45), a candle, and any symbol of Mary, the mother of Jesus.

LEADER: May the peace and love of Jesus be with us today as we gather to talk to God and to listen to God's messages to us.

ALL: May the peace and love of Jesus be with us.

LEADER: During Advent we often hear about Mary, the mother of Jesus. The Gospel stories tell us that she was chosen by God for her special role, and that she received a message from God about it.

Mary wasn't surprised that God should speak to her because she often practiced listening to God. When she realized what God was asking, she simply answered: Whatever you want me to do, my God, I will do it.

Shortly after she found out that she was going to have a baby, she went to visit her cousin Elizabeth who was also pregnant. Here's how Elizabeth greeted Mary:

READER: A reading from the Gospel of Luke:

When Elizabeth heard Mary
call out in greeting,
the baby in her womb jumped.
Elizabeth realized at that moment
that even her baby knew there was
something special about Mary.
Filled with the Holy Spirit,

Elizabeth cried out to Mary:
Blessed are you among women
and blessed is the baby you are carrying.
The moment your greeting
sounded in my ears,
the baby in my womb jumped for joy.
Blessed are you Mary
for trusting in God's word to you!

This is the Word of the Lord.

ALL: Thanks be to God.

LEADER: For 2000 years Christians have retold this story, and Mary has become a model of how we should listen to God and trust in God's words to us. In fact, the church has even composed a prayer based on this story. The prayer is called the Hail Mary.

(It might be appropriate at this point to go through the first part of the prayer line by line, rephrasing it in contemporary terms so the children will understand what it means. You might paraphrase it in this way: "Hello Mary. God has blessed you in a special way, and is always with you. Of all women, you are the most special, and the baby you are carrying is also especially blessed by God. In fact, the baby you are carrying is Jesus." You might also explain that the second half of the prayer is not from Scripture. It is a response later added.)

LEADER: We will say this prayer together during each of our Advent classes. It will remind us that we, too, can listen to God in prayer as we prepare to celebrate the birth of Jesus at Christmas.

LEADER: (Now ask students to repeat the Hail Mary after you, line by line.)

Hail Mary, full of grace,

ALL: Hail Mary, full of grace,

LEADER: The Lord is with you.

ALL: The Lord is with you.

LEADER: Blessed are you among women,

ALL: Blessed are you among women,

LEADER: And blessed is the fruit of your womb, Jesus.

ALL: And blessed is the fruit of your womb, Jesus.

LEADER: Holy Mary, Mother of God,

ALL: Holy Mary, Mother of God,

LEADER: Pray for us sinners,

ALL: Pray for us sinners,

LEADER: Now and at the hour of our death.

ALL: Now and at the hour of our death.

LEADER: Amen.

ALL: Amen.

(Before closing, spend two minutes in silent prayer.)

Celebrating Our Winter Gifts
WE PRAY WITH OUR EARTH

Note: This service can be used from November to March, depending on the weather in your area. It is intended to help children realize that all things (all seasons) are times for prayer.

To Prepare: Assemble in your prayer space several items that represent winter in your area. You might include a bare tree branch, a pair of mittens or gloves, ski goggles, a picture of a snow scene, a dried grape vine, a sprig of evergreen, a piece of holly, etc. Also place there a Bible (open to Psalm 147), and a piece of paper and pencil for each participant.

LEADER: All praise and honor to you, Lord Jesus Christ. We gather here in your name and we believe that you are with us.

ALL: Thanks be to God.

LEADER: Our God is a God of love who has created us and watches over us. God has given us many gifts and one of these gifts is nature. At this time of year we see the cold face of nature. Sometimes the cold is made beautiful by snow; but sometimes it is accompanied by chilling winds and rain.

Sometimes the cold goes right through us and we long for the warm sunshine of other seasons. But even in the cold of winter, God is actively caring for the earth. Let us now listen to a reflection about winter from God's Word, the Bible.

READER: A reading from Psalm 147:

God gives a command to the earth,
And what God says is quickly done.
Snow is spread out like a blanket,

And frost is scattered like ashes.
God sends hail that is as hard as gravel,
And the cold can be almost unbearable.
But then God gives another command,
And the ice melts.
God sends the spring winds,
And spring waters flow once again.
God speaks to us through our earth,
And thus we see God's power and might.
May our God be praised forever!

This is the Word of the Lord.

ALL: Thanks be to God.

LEADER: Winter means something different for each of us. Some of us love the cold, and others wish it would go away. Some love the snow and the ice, and others can't wait until it's gone. It's important that each of us talk to God about our feelings honestly and in our own way.

Let us take time now to write our own personal prayer about winter. This can remind us that God is with us through all the seasons, in good times and bad. All the seasons can be times for praising God.

(Distribute the papers and pencils and allow five minutes or so for the prayer-writing. Also write your own prayer. When all have finished, ask children to hold up their prayers as you say the closing prayer:)

LEADER: We praise you, our God. Please accept the prayers we have written and continue to bless us as we celebrate your presence in winter. Thank you for your winter blessings. Amen.

Remembering Valentine's Day
LOVE IS OUR GOAL

Note: We often tell children that they must love one another. Sometimes their notions of how to do this are very vague. Before praying this service, spend some time discussing actual, concrete ways children can show love for others.

To Prepare: In your prayer space, have a Bible (open to 1 Corinthians 13: 4-7), a candle, pieces of paper for each participant, and pencils or markers. Also have a large cutout heart with enough space inside for all to sign their names. At the bottom of the heart, print the words: "God Is Love."

LEADER: Holy, holy, holy Lord, God of hosts, heaven and earth are filled with your glory. Blessed is the one who comes in the name of the Lord.

ALL: Hosanna in the highest.

LEADER: Our God is a holy God, and we know from the Bible that the greatest sign of holiness is love. But what is love?

READER ONE: Is love what we feel
for our favorite cereal, or our best toy,
or our most expensive piece of clothing?

READER TWO: Is love like having a crush on somebody,
or something people can fall in
every time they meet someone new?

READER THREE: Is love what we feel for people
who do good things for us,
as long as they don't ask
anything in return?

LEADER: The love that comes from God is much more than
these. True love is willing to give, as well as to
receive. True love is unselfish because
it demands nothing in return. Let us now listen to
what Saint Paul told the Christians at Corinth
about the kind of love that comes from God:

READER FOUR: Love is patient; love is kind.
Love is not jealous, it does not show off,
it is not snobbish.
Love is never rude, it is not self-seeking,
it is not prone to anger;
neither does it hold grudges.
Love does not rejoice in what is wrong,
but rejoices with what is right and true.
There is no limit to what love can accept,
no limit to its trust, or its hope,
or its power to keep going.
There are in the end three things that last:
faith, hope, and love,
and the greatest of these is love.

This is the Word of the Lord.

ALL: Thanks be to God.

LEADER: After hearing Paul's words, I invite you now to write a sentence about love. What in your words is the best definition or description of love?

(Hand out papers and pencils for this activity. Also write a definition yourself. When all have finished, continue as follows:)

(picking up the heart) After this service, we will display and share our definitions of love. But first I invite each of you to come forward to write your name within this heart. Your signature will be a sign that you are willing to show the kind of love that is "of God," the kind of love Saint Paul described in his letter to the Christians in Corinth. (Begin by signing your own name. After all have signed, display the heart in clear view of all in the group. Then say the closing prayer together.)

LEADER: Holy, holy, holy Lord, God of hosts, heaven and earth are filled with your glory. Blessed is the one who comes in the name of the Lord.

ALL: Hosanna in the highest.

(Allow time now for sharing definitions or descriptions of love.)

WE CARRY OUR CROSSES

Note: Use this service anytime during the six weeks of Lent. You might want to use the paper cross described below as a focal point for all your lenten prayers.

To Prepare: In or near your prayer space hang a large drawing of a cross, beneath which these words are written: "We Want to Follow Jesus." Have small slips of paper and pencils for each participant as well as a roll of tape. Also place there a Bible (open to Luke 23: 44-47), and a candle.

LEADER: Glory and praise to you, Lord Jesus Christ. We greet you with love, and we ask that you help us listen carefully to your words.

ALL: Amen.

LEADER: We are now in the season of Lent. This is a six-week period when the whole church focuses on the key events in the life of Jesus. During these weeks we are invited to think about things that Jesus said and did, and to ponder their meaning.

We move together during Lent toward Good Friday, the day on which Jesus died on the cross, and we move from there to Easter Sunday and beyond, where we experience Jesus as our risen savior.

READER ONE: During Lent, with our eyes on Jesus,
we try to spend more time at prayer,
more time talking to God
and listening to God.

READER TWO: During Lent, with our eyes on Jesus,
we try to be more aware
of the needs of others,
and to share our time and our money
with the poor, the hungry, and the homeless.

READER THREE: During Lent, with our eyes on Jesus,
we try to grow stronger as persons
by learning to say no to our sins
and our failings,
and by sometimes even saying no
to the things we enjoy.

LEADER: With our eyes on Jesus, we journey through Lent trying to understand and accept what God has in store for us. Jesus did this, and he is our example. Even as he died, Jesus gave himself over to whatever God wanted of him. Let us listen now to a description of his death on the cross:

READER FOUR: A reading from the Gospel of Luke:

It was about noontime, but darkness
(like that from an eclipse of the sun)
had settled over the whole land.
This lasted until mid-afternoon.
Jesus, having been
on the cross three hours,
uttered a loud cry and said:
Father, into your hands
I give over my spirit.
After he said this, he died.
Upon seeing what had happened,
a soldier gave glory to God and cried out:
Surely this was an innocent man.

This is the Word of the Lord.

ALL: Thanks be to God.

LEADER: Let us now reflect for a few moments about what we have just heard. Close your eyes and speak to Jesus in your own words about how you will use this special time called Lent.

(Allow two to three minutes of silence for this.)

I will now distribute small slips of paper on which you can write a word or two to describe how you will try to become a better person this Lent. We will attach these to the paper cross on our prayer table and display it.

(Allow time for writing and then have participants come forward one at a time to attach their papers to the cross. Decide together where you will hang it.)

Preparing for Reconciliation
TIME TO SAY "I'M SORRY"

Note: Children preparing for First Reconciliation would benefit from this service. Explain to them beforehand, however, that this is not actually the sacrament of reconciliation. Rather, it is a reminder that we can offer one another peace and forgiveness anytime, anywhere.

You might also want to use this service when there has been discord in your group, whenever you sense that it's time for children to say "I'm sorry" to one another.

Finally, Lent is certainly an appropriate time to reflect with children on the need all of us have for the peace and forgiveness of Jesus.

To Prepare: Place on your prayer table a Bible (open to John 20:20-23), a bowl of holy water, a small sprig of evergreen, and verse cards for each participant on which are written the words: "Peace be with you."

LEADER: Coming together as God's children, let us remember that God is full of gentleness and compassion for us. God knows us as we are, our good points and our weak ones. God strengthens us to do good, but also forgives us when we fail.

READER ONE: For the times that we forget
that we are brothers and sisters
who should respect one another
and help one another,
Lord, have mercy.

ALL: Lord, have mercy.

READER TWO: For the times that we act selfishly,

putting our own concerns
before those of others,
Christ, have mercy.

ALL: Christ, have mercy.

READER THREE: For the times we have hurt one another
with our angry words or actions,
Lord, have mercy.

ALL: Lord, have mercy.

LEADER: No matter what we have done, Jesus offers us
the chance to try again. Peter, one of his first
followers, failed Jesus completely. When Jesus
was arrested, Peter denied three times that he
even knew him. But Jesus forgave Peter's weak-
ness and gave him the chance to begin again. Listen now to how Jesus greeted his followers,
including Peter, after his resurrection.

READER FOUR: A reading from the Gospel of John:

On the first day of the week,
the disciples met together
with the doors locked
because they were afraid.
Jesus came and stood among them,
and he said, "Peace be with you."
Then he showed them
his hands and his side,
and when they understood
that it was really Jesus,
the disciples were full of joy.
Jesus said to them again:

"Peace be with you!"

This is the Word of the Lord.

ALL: Thanks be to God.

(Invite children to stand in a circle. Ask one child to carry the bowl of water as you hold the sprig of evergreen and move from child to child to lightly sprinkle each with the holy water. As you do so, say the following blessing:
"_____, may you receive the peace and forgiveness of Jesus."
Return to the prayer table and pick up the verse cards. Explain that Jesus speaks the same words to us today that he spoke to Peter and the other first followers. These cards are a reminder of this greeting. Present one to each child individually.)

LEADER: Let us now resolve to love and forgive one another, and let us offer one another this greeting of peace:

"The peace of Christ be with you."

(Ask all to reply to one another:
"And also with you.")

Having Faith and Trust
GOD TAKES CARE OF US

Note: This service emphasizes our need to place ourselves in God's hands, and thus, it can be used at any time of the year. Because it uses bread and wine, it might also be used to prepare for the sacrament of the Eucharist.

To Prepare: Place on your prayer table a Bible (open to Luke 12:20-34), a plate of bread (a small piece for each participant), a jug of grape juice, and small paper cups, one for each child.

LEADER: Blessed are you, Lord God of all creation. Through your goodness we have bread to offer, which earth has given and human hands have made. It will become for us the Bread of Life.

ALL: Blessed be God forever.

LEADER: Blessed are you, Lord God of all creation.
Through your goodness we have wine to offer,
fruit of the vine and work of human hands.
It will become our spiritual drink.

ALL: Blessed be God forever.

LEADER: Blessed are you, Lord God, for you nourish us,
too, with your Word. Open our hearts and minds
as we now listen.

READER: A reading from the Gospel of Luke:

Jesus said these words to the people:
I tell you, you shouldn't worry about life,
wondering what you're going to eat
or what you're going to wear.
Think of the birds outside.
They don't worry about these things,
and yet God feeds them.
And look at the flowers in the fields.
They don't worry either,
and yet they are more beautiful
than a king's finest robes.
When you put your mind on God
and the things of God,
everything else will be taken care of.

This is the Word of the Lord.

ALL: Thanks be to God.

LEADER: Let us pray. God, we ask you to help us not to
worry. Help us to believe that you will take care
of us because you love us and guide us always.
Teach us not to trust in money and all the things

it can buy, but to trust in you instead.

(Ask all to answer "Teach us how to trust in you" to the following petitions:)

LEADER: Help us not to worry about having snack foods and drinks, but rather to consider sharing our food and drink with those in need.

ALL: Teach us how to trust in you.

LEADER: Help us not to worry about wearing expensive clothes, but rather to share our clothing with those who have far less than we do.

ALL: Teach us how to trust in you.

(Invite children to pray spontaneously about additional "worries" they may have. After these petitions, continue as follows:)

LEADER: As a sign of his love and care, Jesus asked us to break bread together and to share wine together in memory of him. We do this every week in our Eucharistic liturgy. Let us now share these gifts in class as a reminder of the presence of Jesus. May they help us to remember that God takes care of us.

(Explain to the children that this sharing is only a symbol and reminder of what we do at our Eucharistic liturgies. Then pass each child a piece of bread and a cup of juice saying: "_____, remember that God takes care of you." Conclude by inviting children to offer one another a sign of peace.)

JESUS IS RISEN! ALLELUIA

Note: This is obviously an Easter service, but recall that the Easter season lasts for 50 days. It is appropriate to use this service throughout that time.

To Prepare: In your prayer space, place a Bible (open to Luke 24: 1-8), a candle, and flowers or other symbols of spring (or new life).

LEADER: May the peace of the risen Jesus be with you.

ALL: And also with you.

LEADER: What must it have been like to be one of the women going to the tomb of Jesus on Easter morning? They wanted to anoint the dead body of Jesus with special oils and perfumes, as was the custom at that time. They couldn't do this on Friday for it was against the law to perform these rituals on the Sabbath (sundown Friday through sundown Saturday). I wonder what the women were thinking and saying as they went along...

READER ONE: I'll feel a lot better
once we have anointed Jesus' body.
The least someone deserves
is the proper burial ceremonies!
I only wish we could
have done it Friday evening.
To think of Jesus
in that tomb unanointed...

READER TWO: Well at least we're doing it
at the crack of dawn.
As soon as we're done,
I'll stop by to tell Mary.
She'll rest easier knowing,
and I'm glad we could do it for her.

READER THREE: She's been through so much.
My only concern is how
we're going to get that stone moved.
It took four soldiers to push it into place.
Maybe we could use a wedge somehow.
Or maybe some of the soldiers
are still hanging around.
We'll just have to see when we get there.

LEADER: When the women got to the tomb, they found the stone already rolled away, so they went in; but they did not find the body of Jesus. They stood there puzzled about this, when suddenly two messengers in bright shining clothes stood by them. Full of fear, the women bowed down to the ground, but the messengers gave them some great news.

READER FOUR: Why are you looking among the dead
for one who is alive?
Jesus is not here; he has been raised.
Remember what he said to you
while he was in Galilee:
The Son of Man must be
handed over and crucified,
and three days later
he will be raised to new life.

LEADER: The women did remember these words. They rushed back to the disciples and Mary, the mother of Jesus, to share this good news. Imagine how excited everyone must have been. What could it mean that the body was gone? Who were the messengers? Where was Jesus?

All of these answers would eventually unfold, and even today we celebrate these events. We share the joyous discovery that Jesus is risen. Let us now offer one another a sign of peace using these words:

"May the peace of the risen Jesus be with you."

Please respond to one another:

"And also with you."

(If you have enough flowers or other symbols of spring, distribute one to each child with these words:

"_____, accept this sign of spring. May it remind you of the risen Jesus.")

WE ARE FILLED WITH THE SPIRIT

Note: This Pentecost service focuses on the presence of the Holy Spirit. Remind children before the service that in order to stay among us, Jesus sent us his Spirit. Allow sufficient time for questions and/or discussion about what this means.

To Prepare: In your prayer space, set up a table on which is placed a Bible (open to Acts 2: 1-4), a candle, and pre-cut "tongues of fire" (flames), one for each participant. On a large piece of posterboard, write the words "We are filled with the Holy Spirit," and place this, too, on the table.

LEADER: Glory be to the Father, and to the Son, and to the Holy Spirit...

ALL: As it was in the beginning, is now, and ever shall be, world without end. Amen.

LEADER: After his resurrection, Jesus was "taken up to heaven." At his request, his followers were to wait together in prayer for a sign from him. This sign would assure them that Jesus would be with them always. They probably had no clear idea about what to expect or when to expect it.

This is how God's Word, the Bible, describes the sign that Jesus sent:

READER ONE: A reading from the Acts of the Apostles:

All the believers were
gathered together in one place.
Suddenly there was a noise from the sky
that sounded like a strong wind blowing,
and it filled the whole house
where they were sitting.
Then they saw what looked like
tongues of fire that spread out
and touched each person there.
They were all filled with the Holy Spirit
and began to talk in other languages
as the Spirit taught them to speak.

This is the Word of the Lord.

ALL: Thanks be to God.

READER TWO: The sign sent by Jesus was the Holy Spirit.
And who was this Holy Spirit
but the Spirit of Jesus himself!
Jesus would now be with his followers,
not in his earthly form,
but through the Holy Spirit.

READER THREE: Those first followers immediately
felt the effects of the Holy Spirit.
And today followers of Jesus, like us,

continue to feel the presence
of the Holy Spirit.
According to the promise of Jesus,
the Holy Spirit is among us
whenever we gather in the name of Jesus.
We don't see the Holy Spirit,
but we can believe in the promise of Jesus;
we can believe that Jesus is with us.

LEADER: To express our faith in the presence of Jesus, let us now write our names on the flames I will distribute. In addition to your name, also write a word or phrase that expresses your belief in the presence of Jesus (for example: Amen, I believe, Alleluia, Thanks Jesus, etc.).

(Allow time for this activity, and then invite children to come forward one at a time to attach their flame to the posterboard. When all the flames are in place, continue as follows:)

Let us now join hands and pray:

LEADER: Glory Be to the Father, and to the Son, and to the Holy Spirit...

ALL: As it was in the beginning, is now, and ever shall be, world without end. Amen.

(After the prayer, decide together where you will keep your "Spirit" poster. Or, ask the children if they would like to "take turns" displaying the poster in their homes.)

Preparing for Vacation
GOD GIVES US SUMMER GIFTS

Note: This service can be prayed anytime before your summer break. It reminds children that learning about God never stops and that there are many summer reminders of the presence of God.

To Prepare: On your prayer table, place several symbols of summer, a Bible (open to Ephesians 5: 8-14), a candle, and small cards for each child on which are printed the words: "Remember God's presence and love—all summer."

LEADER: Looking forward to summer is a happy time for all of us. But we want to be certain not to forget all that we have learned about Jesus and his teachings. During this prayer time, we will think about some summer things that can remind us of Jesus.

(Ask children to suggest things that might remind them of Jesus during the summer. What things might speak to them of his presence?)

LEADER: One of my favorite reminders of Jesus' presence is the sun. The summer sun is bright and hot, and it speaks to me of God's power. The sun's rays remind me of God's love reaching out to me. The light of the sun reminds me that Jesus is the light of the world. God's Word reminds us to walk in this light. Let's listen.

READER: A reading from the letter to the Ephesians:

There was a time
when you were in darkness,
but now you are light in the Lord.
Well then, live as children of light.
Light produces every kind of goodness
and also justice and truth…

Awake, O sleepers, arise,
and Christ will give you light.

This is the Word of the Lord.

ALL: Thanks be to God.

LEADER: There are many other summer signs of God's
presence and love. Some of them are on our
prayer table. But some are too big to bring inside,
like lakes and oceans, and fields of flowers, and
vegetable gardens, and the millions of grains of
sand on the seashore. All of these things can
speak to us of God's presence and love.
   I have made a card for each of you to help you
remember Jesus when you see these things. Place
it someplace in your room at home where you
will see it every day during the summer.

(Call each child forward by name, one at a time,
and present the verse cards from the prayer table.
Conclude as below:)

LEADER: Let us remember that God loves and cares for us
and gives us many special summer gifts. Each
time you see one of these gifts, offer a prayer of
thanks. Let us thank God together now.

For sun and clouds and bright blue days,
we thank you, God.

ALL: We thank you, God.

LEADER: For water and sand and gigantic waves,
we thank you, God.

ALL: We thank you, God.

LEADER: For all your summer gifts,
and for your love and care for us,
we thank you, God.

ALL: We thank you, God.

LEADER: God, our loving parent, and Jesus, our brother
and friend, watch over us this summer and keep
us in your loving care. Amen.

ALL: Amen.

Celebrating Someone's Special Day
A BIRTHDAY BLESSING

Note: Obviously, this is a service that celebrates the individual birthdays of your class or group. At the beginning of the year, obtain a list of all birth dates and celebrate each with this service as close to the actual date as possible.

To Prepare: Place a Bible on your prayer table (open to Paul's letter to the Philippians), a lighted candle, and a large poster drawing of a birthday cake. Put the birthday child's name somewhere on the poster.

LEADER: Blessed are you, God of all creation.

ALL: Blessed are you forever.

LEADER: We thank you for the gifts you have given us, our God, especially for gifts of food and drink, for our homes and our families, and for all our friends. Today we especially thank you for our friend,_____, whose birthday it is.

READER ONE: We thank you, God, for the gift of life
you have given_____.
We ask your blessing upon _____
that she (he) might continue
to honor and praise you
by using the gifts and talents
you have given her (him).
We wish for her (him) to continue growing in
age, wisdom, and grace—as Jesus grew.

READER TWO: We wish for_____,
this blessing from God's Word, the Bible
(adapted from Paul's letter
to the Christians in Philippi:)

We thank our God for you
whenever we think of you....

Our prayer for you is that
you might have God's love in you
so that you can make
the best possible choices in your life.
We pray that you will live
a life of goodness
and that you may always
give praise and glory to God.

This is the Word of the Lord.

ALL: Thanks be to God.

LEADER: We thank you, God, for _____, and we
ask your continued blessing upon her (him).

(Invite all to extend their hands in blessing in the
direction of the birthday person.)

May you always have God's love in you.

ALL: Amen.

LEADER: May you always make good choices in your life.

ALL: Amen.

LEADER: May you continue to grow in age, in wisdom,
and in grace—as Jesus did.

ALL: Amen.

LEADER: _____, I now invite you to come
forward, to receive a blessing of peace.

(Make the Sign of the Cross on the child's
forehead while saying, "Peace be with you."
Invite all the children to do the same.)

Mourning the Death of a Pet
ALL CREATURES ARE GOD'S

Note: This service can be done spontaneously, whenever a child shares sorrow over the death of a pet. Before praying together, you might want to let the children talk about what they think happens to a pet when it dies. Explain that God cares for all created things and continues to extend this care even when a creature returns to the earth (in other words, dies).

To Prepare: On a large piece of posterboard print the words: "We all belong to God." Place this somewhere in clear view. Light a small candle and place it on your prayer table.

LEADER: Today during our prayer time we are going to think about and talk about a wonderful gift that God has created for us, the gift of pets. And then we are going to talk to God about how we feel when we lose one of our pets.

Close your eyes for a minute and think about these questions; don't answer out loud, just answer in your own head:

•Do you have a pet?

•Have you ever had one?

•Does someone you know have a pet that you play with?

•How do pets make you feel?

(After this quiet time, instruct Reader One to begin. Instruct all other children to respond: "Thank you, God, for pets.")

READER ONE:　Let us together thank God
for pets we have ourselves,
or pets that belong
to our friends and neighbors.
Thank you, God, for pets.

ALL:　Thank you, God, for pets.

READER TWO:　Thank you, God, for dogs and cats,
for birds and fish,
and for all your creatures.
Thank you for the joy pets give us.

ALL:　Thank you, God, for pets.

READER THREE:　Thank you, God, for caring for us
and watching over us.
Thank you, too, for caring for our pets.
Help us to know that even when they die,
our pets are still in your care.
Thank you, God, for pets.

ALL:　Thank you, God, for pets.

LEADER:　Now close your eyes again and think about
these questions:

•Has one of your pets ever died?

•Have you known someone whose pet has died?

•How did you feel when this happened?

(After a brief period of silence continue
as follows:)

Dear God, pets make us happy, but we feel very sad when one of them dies.

Today, _____ is very sad because his (her) pet has died. We know that you care for us, God, and we believe that you care for all living things.

Please help _____ not to be too sad. Help him (her) to remember the good and fun times he (she) had with this pet.

LEADER: (Invite children to spend some time now talking to God about their own feelings about pets.)

Thank you, God, for all the good times we have with our pets. Help us to quickly get over our sadness when they die, and to remember them with love and thanksgiving.

ALL: Thank you, God, for pets.

(Now invite the child whose pet has died to come forward to print his or her name and the name of his or her pet at the top of the poster. Then invite all the other children to also come forward to print their names andthe name of a pet [their own or someone else's] somewhere on the poster.)

Taking Care of Our Bodies

GOD WANTS US HEALTHY

Note: Before beginning this service, ask children what they think God wants of them. They will probably answer: To love others, obey parents and teachers, be good. Explain, however, that God also wants them to take care of themselves.

Remind children that even adults sometimes forget that their bodies are a special gift that need care. This service will reflect on the importance of keeping healthy—as God wants us to be.

To Prepare: Place on your prayer table a Bible (open to Psalm 27: 13-14), a candle, and if possible, also have a large bowl (or other container) of fruit, one piece or serving for each child. (You might want to request beforehand in a note to parents that each child bring a piece of fruit for this service.)

LEADER: In the Bible, there are many sayings about growing strong in our faith, but we can't grow strong in our hearts and minds unless our bodies, too, are strong. Listen to this reading (adapted) from Psalm 27, a song-prayer from the Bible:

READER ONE: This I believe:
I will see the goodness of God
in this land of the living.
But I must put my hope in God,
and I must keep my body strong.
I will try to have courage
and to place my trust in God.

This is the Word of the Lord.

ALL: Thanks be to God.

LEADER: When Jesus was a boy, perhaps he sometimes

prayed this song-prayer. The Bible says that Jesus grew strong and healthy in three ways: 1) in age, 2) in what he understood about life (wisdom), and 3) in his love and closeness to God (grace). We, too, are called by God to grow in these ways. Today, we are going to ask God to help us grow in the first way.

(Here ask the children to suggest ways that they can keep healthy as they grow in age.)

We all know that one way we can grow strong in our bodies is to eat the right foods. God has created us, and God has also created foods to nourish us.

(Ask the children which foods are the most nourishing and which help us to grow healthy.)

LEADER: Some of you knew right away that fruit is one particular food that will help us to grow healthy. We have some fruit here today, and so we will have a "blessing of the fruit" ceremony. Then we will share some of this special food.

READER TWO: God has given us
many different kinds of fruit.
They have different shapes and colors,
and they all have different tastes.
Thank you, God, for fruit.
We praise you for this
wonderful gift you have created.

LEADER: (Invite all to extend their right hands toward the bowl of fruit as you pray the following blessings:)

Thank you, God, for apples, red ones, yellow
ones, and green ones. Blessed are you for
creating them.

ALL: We praise and thank you, God.

LEADER: Thank you, God, for oranges and tangerines, for
lemons and limes, and for grapefruit. Blessed are
you for creating them.

ALL: We praise and thank you, God.

LEADER: Thank you, God, for bananas and grapes,
and for kiwi fruit and cherries.
Blessed are you for creating them.

ALL: We praise and thank you, God.

LEADER: Thank you, God, for peaches and pears,
and for plums and nectarines.
Blessed are you for creating them.

ALL: We praise and thank you, God.

LEADER: For all your special gifts to us,
we praise and thank you, God.

ALL: We praise and thank you, God. Amen.

(Now share and enjoy the fruit.)

Celebrating Our Faith

A SPECIAL GIFT FROM GOD

Note: This service can be used at any time of the year. It can be used with any lesson or story about faith.

To Prepare: In your prayer space, place a Bible (open to 1 Timothy 6:11-16), a candle, and a large poster in the shape of a shield, on which are printed these words: "Faith is a gift from God."

LEADER: The peace of Christ be with you.

ALL: And also with you.

LEADER: May the love of God be in our hearts and minds as we gather to pray.

ALL: Amen. So be it. Amen.

LEADER: We have received the gift of faith from our God.
Sometimes this gift is very hard to practice
because we get messages from the world around
us that are different from God's message.
It has always been this way. The early Christians,
too, had to struggle against the messages of their
culture. Listen now to what the apostle Paul
wrote to his friend Timothy:

READER ONE: You are the chosen ones of God,
and you must flee from the evil
that surrounds you.
Try to be honest in everything you do.
Use the gifts of piety, faith, love,
and faithfulness that God has given you.
Be gentle and understanding
with one another.
Continue to fight the good fight of faith.

This is the Word of the Lord.

ALL: Thanks be to God.

LEADER: Let us now pray to our God that we might
continue to practice our faith, no matter what
other messages we hear.

READER TWO: That we might help one another
to understand God's message,
let us pray to the Lord...

ALL: Lord, hear our prayer.

READER THREE: That we might make good use
of our gifts from God,
let us pray to the Lord...

ALL: Lord, hear our prayer.

READER FOUR: That we might deal with one another
in gentle and loving ways,
let us pray to the Lord...

ALL: Lord, hear our prayer.

READER FIVE: That we might help one another
to grow strong in our faith,
let us pray to the Lord...

ALL: Lord, hear our prayer.

LEADER: (Invite children to comment on what "messages"
they hear in our culture today that are contrary to
what God asks of them. Ask for suggestions
about how these messages might be resisted.
Then continue as follows:)

I invite you to come forward now, one at a time,
for a blessing.

(As each comes forward, say:

"_____, continue to grow in
your faith."

When all have received a blessing, recite the
following closing prayer:)

LEADER: May God, who has given us the gift of faith,
be with us and guide us. To our God be honor
and praise forever.

ALL: Amen. So be it. Amen.

WE CARE FOR THE EARTH

Note: The purpose of this service is to help children become aware of their responsibility to care for the earth. It can be used on Arbor Day, Earth Day, or at any time during the year.

To Prepare: Set up a special prayer table "exhibit" that contains these items: a container of water, rocks, soil, a plant, and any other items that symbolize "earth" for you.

LEADER: May the peace of our Lord,
Jesus Christ, be with you.

ALL: And also with you.

LEADER: May the peace of our Lord, Jesus Christ, also be upon our earth. The earth is God's creation, but it has been damaged and disturbed by all of us, the people who dwell within it.

READER ONE: (holding up the water:)
May the peace of Jesus
be upon our waters:
our oceans and rivers,
lakes and streams.
We have polluted our waterways and caused harm to all the life forms in them. Let us resolve to watch over the waters that God has created. We thank you, God, for our waterways.

ALL: Thank you, God, for our waterways.

READER TWO: (holding up a rock:)
May the peace of Jesus be upon this rock and upon all the rocks and stone

that are beneath our earth.
We have disturbed this rock to build
our roads and homes and businesses.
Let us resolve to respect
what remains of earth's rock
and to use it with care.
We thank you, God, for rocks and stone.

ALL: Thank you, God, for rocks and stone.

READER THREE: (holding up the soil:)
May the peace of Jesus be upon this soil and
upon all the soil throughout the world
in which is planted seeds
for food and survival.
We have damaged the soil
with chemicals and nuclear waste,
and such damage cannot be undone.
Let us resolve to care for the soil
that it may be safe
for plants and trees and grass.
Thank you, God, for the gift of soil.

ALL: Thank you, God, for the gift of soil.

READER FOUR: (holding up the plant:)
May the peace of Jesus be upon this plant
and upon all the plants, flowers,
shrubs, and trees on our earth.
Many of our vital plants have been
destroyed to make way for roads and buildings.
Let us resolve to respect
the plants of the earth
and to value the contributions
they make to life.

We thank you, God, for plants.

ALL: We thank you, God, for plants.

LEADER: Let us now spend a few moments in silent prayer. Let us ask God to protect our earth from further damage and destruction, and to teach us how to treat the earth with love and respect.

(Allow three minutes for silent prayer and reflection.)

LEADER: Let us pray. God, our creator, we ask you in a special way today to teach us how to love and preserve our mother earth. This is one of your greatest gifts to us. May we offer the earth only love and peace. We ask this through Jesus Christ, your son, our Lord.

ALL: Amen.

WE CAN BE SAINTS

Note: Though this is an All Saints' Day service, you might also consider using it on the feastdays of saints that are special to your class, group, or parish. Beforehand, ask children to bring to this service some symbol of their name saint or a favorite saint. If they can't think of a symbol, have them bring a paper banner with a saint's name on it.

To Prepare: On your prayer table, place a Bible (open to Isaiah 2:1-5), and a candle. Leave room for the symbols or banners the children have brought. Invite children to move out of the room (taking their symbols or banners with them), so you can re-enter in procession to your prayer area. Before starting the procession, ask Reader One to begin as below.

READER ONE: A reading from the Book of Isaiah:

The mountain of the Lord's house
shall be established
as the highest mountain
and be raised above the hills.
All peoples and all nations
shall stream toward it.
Many peoples will come and say:
Let us climb the Lord's mountain
to the house of our God,
that we may be instructed in God's ways,
and walk in God's paths....
Come, let us walk in the light of the Lord.

This is the Word of the Lord.

ALL: Thanks be to God.

(Now walk in procession together to your prayer

space, with the children holding high their symbols or banners. When they reach the prayer table, have them place their symbols on it and then form a circle around the table.)

LEADER: We have come in procession to the table of the Lord to be instructed in God's ways and to walk in God's path. We do this in imitation of the saints who have walked in procession toward God all their lives. They opened their minds and hearts to God's Word, so they could understand what God was asking of them. Let us now in silence open our minds and hearts to God. Let us listen for God's instruction.

(Allow a minute or so for silent prayer.)

READER TWO: That all the saints
represented here on this table,
might pray to God on our behalf,
let us pray to the Lord...

ALL: Lord, hear our prayer.

READER THREE: That all the saints
might teach us how to
climb the mountain of the Lord,
let us pray to the Lord...

ALL: Lord, hear our prayer.

READER FOUR: That all the saints
might teach us to walk in God's paths,
in the light of the Lord,
let us pray to the Lord...

ALL: Lord, hear our prayer.

(Encourage children to pray spontaneous prayers of petition through the intercession of their name saints. When all who wish have prayed, continue as below:)

LEADER: Remembering that the saints speak to God for us, let us now join them in spirit as we hold hands and pray to God our Father:

ALL: Our Father, who art in heaven,
hallowed be thy name.
Thy kingdom come,
thy will be done,
on earth as it is in heaven.
Give us this day our daily bread,
and forgive us our trespasses
as we forgive those who
trespass against us.
And lead us not into temptation,
but deliver us from evil.
Amen.

Shouting Our Thanks
NATURE IS FROM GOD

Note: The object of this service is to help children focus on the things in nature that God has created. Discuss with them beforehand what "things in nature" the Pilgrims and the Indians might have been grateful for.

Invite them to bring to this service a symbol of some created thing for which they are particularly grateful. Or invite them to draw a picture of something they enjoy in nature.

To Prepare: Have the children walk in procession to your prayer space, holding high their nature symbols or drawings. When they reach the prayer space, invite them to place what they are carrying on the prayer table. Place a lighted candle in the center.

LEADER: Together let us "shout out" our praise to God for all the wonderful things in nature that we enjoy. Sometimes we forget that things like sunshine, flowers, clouds, grass, water, sand, and snow are all gifts from God.

LEADER: (In a loud voice:)
Let us praise God for all the gifts of nature.

ALL: Let us praise God for all the gifts of nature.

LEADER: We give you thanks, God of all creation, for your gifts...

•for the gifts of sun, moon, and stars...

ALL: We give you thanks.

•for the wind and the water,

the beach and the sand…

ALL: We give you thanks.

•for the clouds in the sky,
for sunrises and sunsets…

ALL: We give you thanks.

•for the gift of rain that waters the earth…

ALL: We give you thanks.

•for birds and fish, and all
the creatures of the sea and sky…

ALL: We give you thanks.

•for wild animals and tame animals,
for caterpillars and frogs,
for insects and butterflies…

ALL: We give you thanks.

•for turkeys and for the fruits
and grains of the land…

ALL: We give you thanks.

LEADER: (Invite children to add to this list some of the things in nature they enjoy.)

•Let us praise God for all these gifts of nature.

ALL: Let us praise God for all these gifts of nature.

LEADER: We ask you, God, to help us value and take care of the gifts you have given us. Help us to keep our earth safe and clean. Thank you for all the gifts you have given us. Amen.

ALL: Thank you for all the gifts you have given us. Amen.

(Invite children to go one by one to the prayer table to pick up their symbols or drawings. Encourage any who wish to do so to tell the others about what they have brought [or drawn]. When all have had a turn, encourage the children to share their symbols [or drawings] with their family members at home.)

Waiting for Jesus in Advent
COME, LORD JESUS

Note: This Advent service, though intended for use before Christmas, can also be used later in the year with groups of children preparing for First Eucharist.

To Prepare: Place on the prayer table a packet of seeds, a container of soil, a Bible (open to James 5: 7-10), and a candle.

LEADER: Peace be with you.

ALL: And also with you.

LEADER: During this season of Advent, we wait and prepare for the birthday of Jesus. Because we know that we will get presents at Christmas, and have parties, and maybe even have company from out of town, it is very hard to wait. So we must have patience. Do you know what patience is? How does it "feel" to be patient? For what jobs must people be very patient?

(Invite children to discuss their concepts of waiting and patience, and to guess which grown-up occupations require the most patience.)

LEADER: Did anyone think of farmers? They are certainly people who could tell us what patience feels like. All winter long they have to wait until the soil is ready again for seeds and plants. And after they plant in spring, they must wait for the seeds to grow and produce.
   Did you know that during Advent, one of the Sunday readings is about farmers (Third Sunday of Advent)? Here's what it says.

READER ONE: A reading from the letter of James:

Be patient my brothers and sisters,
until the coming of the Lord.
Look at the farmers.
See how they wait for their crops to grow
so they can be gathered.
They have to wait patiently while the soil
receives the winter and the spring rains.
You, too, must be patient.
Steady your hearts,
because Jesus is coming soon.
Do not grumble among yourselves,
but instead, practice patience.

This is the Word of the Lord.

ALL: Thanks be to God.

LEADER: Let us now pray to God, our loving parent, as we
wait for the coming of Jesus.

READER TWO: That we might learn from those
who farm the land
how to wait with patience,
let us pray to the Lord...

ALL: Lord, hear our prayer.

READER THREE: That we might use
our Advent waiting time
to prepare our hearts
for the birthday of Jesus,
let us pray to the Lord...

ALL: Lord, hear our prayer.

READER FOUR: That we might remember
when we share gifts on Christmas
that God first shared

the gift of Jesus with us,
let us pray to the Lord...

ALL: Lord, hear our prayer.

READER FIVE: That we might think first of Jesus
on Christmas morning,
remembering that it is his birthday,
let us pray to the Lord...

ALL: Lord, hear our prayer.

LEADER: Let us now add our own prayers to these.

(Invite children to pray for personal or family
needs, or about any concerns they may have.
When all who wish have prayed,
continue as below:)

LEADER: (holding up the packet of seeds and the soil)
God, our loving parent, thank you for Jesus.
Thank you for the farmers who work the land,
and thank you for the gift of patience.
May Jesus come soon.
Come, Lord Jesus, come. Amen.

ALL: Come, Lord Jesus, come. Amen.

Imitating God's Generous Love
JESUS IS BORN AT CHRISTMAS

Note: This service can be prayed anytime during Advent. It is obviously intended to help children reflect upon the true meaning of the Nativity. Sometime before this service, prepare cards for each child on which are printed: "Jesus was born on Christmas day; let us celebrate and rejoice!"

To Prepare: Place on your prayer table a candle, a birthday card, and a wrapped gift (preferably wrapped with birthday paper) in which are the cards you have prepared for the children. (If you are conducting this service a week or so before Christmas, you might want to bake a birthday cake or cupcakes, and these, too, can be placed on the prayer table.)

LEADER: We all love to celebrate our birthdays. Usually on this day we receive presents, and often there is a party to celebrate the day we were born. Our family members and friends are happy that we came into their lives on this day and they rejoice with us.

READER ONE: Jesus was born on Christmas Day.
Who will celebrate with him?
Who will rejoice with him?

LEADER: On December 25th, we celebrate the birthday of Jesus. In our homes on Christmas Day, will it be the birthday of Jesus that we are celebrating? Will we be rejoicing that Jesus was born? Who will get the presents?

READER TWO: Jesus was born on Christmas Day.
Who will celebrate with him?
Who will rejoice with him?

LEADER: Have you ever wondered why we give one

another presents on Christmas? Doesn't it seem strange that we are the ones opening gifts? What about Jesus, whose birthday it is?

(Invite children to offer possible reasons why we are the "gifted" ones.)

LEADER: On Christmas Day we celebrate the greatest gift that God ever gave us. We celebrate the gift of Jesus. In imitation of the generous giving of God, our loving parent, we give one another gifts. It's as if God is saying: This birthday of Jesus is the greatest birthday of all. All of you should celebrate and rejoice, and all of you should get presents.

READER THREE: Jesus was born on Christmas Day.
All of us can celebrate!
All of us can rejoice!

LEADER: Here on our prayer table is a birthday card. Let's take a few minutes to read it, and then all of us can sign it. Even though we can't really mail it to Jesus, it will remind us that Christmas is really his birthday.

(Read the card together. Sign it yourself and then have the children sign it.)

LEADER: (picking up the gift from the prayer table) I wonder who this gift is for? (Randomly choose a child to open it.) It's for all of you from me. Remembering the gift God our Father gave us, I wanted to give each of you a small gift in honor of Jesus' birthday.

(Distribute these in any way you wish and if you have a cake or cupcakes, share these in the same spirit. Before closing, say the following prayer refrain, inviting the children to repeat after you:)

LEADER: Jesus was born on Christmas Day.

ALL: Jesus was born on Christmas Day.

LEADER: All of us can celebrate!

ALL: All of us can celebrate!

LEADER: All of us can rejoice!

ALL: All of us can rejoice!

LEADER: Happy birthday, Jesus. Amen.

ALL: Happy birthday, Jesus. Amen.

Making Wise Choices
GOD GIVES US COURAGE

Note: Most children are familiar with the national campaign to "just say no" to drugs. But there are many other situations in their lives that will also require the courage to say no. This service focuses on the need for children to pray for guidance and strength before they make choices. It can be used at any time of the year, but would be especially appropriate during Lent, for it is then that we particularly focus on changing ourselves for the better.

To Prepare: Place on your prayer table two signs. On one print the words: Yes to God. On the other, print the words: No to Wrong Things. Also, place there a small bowl with oil in it (baby oil, for example). Practice beforehand with the three readers.

LEADER: In many of the stories we read, or in the movies, or on TV, there are heroes or heroines, brave people who must take some action to help or save others. What makes them heroic is that they choose to do what is required, even when it is dangerous to themselves.

(Ask the children if they know of any heroic characters.)

In the Bible there are many people who did very brave things—either because God asked it of them or for the sake of others.

(Again, ask children to name some of these people. If they find this difficult, mention Abraham and Sarah, Moses, David, Mary, the mother of Jesus, Joseph, Paul, any of the many other saints, and, of course, Jesus himself.)

LEADER: Listen now to a story about a follower of Jesus
some of you may not have heard of. His name is
Stephen. He was one of those people who did
something extremely brave for God and
others.

READER ONE: A reading from the Acts of the Apostles:

Stephen was chosen
by the first followers of Jesus
to help them take care of those
who needed food and money.
Stephen did this, but he also sometimes cured
people of their sicknesses,
and he was able to speak wonderfully about
Jesus and his teachings.

READER TWO: This made the leaders
of the synagogue very angry.
They were jealous that so many people
wanted to listen to Stephen,
and so they arrested him on false charges.
When he came before the judge,
Stephen was not afraid.
He bravely gave a speech about God
and how God wanted the people
to believe in Jesus.
But this made the leaders
even more angry.

READER THREE: Stephen's mind and heart were filled
all through with the Holy Spirit.
When he finished his speech,

he looked up into heaven.
He saw the glory of God,
and he saw Jesus himself with God.
"Look," Stephen cried out,
"the heavens are opened
and I can see Jesus standing with God."
When the jealous leaders heard this,
they put their fingers in their ears.
Yelling with fury,
they all rushed at Stephen
and dragged him outside the city
and stoned him.

READER FOUR: Even as they did this,
Stephen prayed,
"Jesus, Lord, receive my spirit,
and forgive these people for their sins."
With these words,
Stephen fell into the sleep of death.

This is the Word of the Lord.

ALL: Thanks be to God.

LEADER: Not too many of us will ever have to die for our choices like Stephen, but there are times in our lives when we need courage to do the right thing.

(Ask children to suggest some situations that call for a great deal of courage on their part.)

Let us now talk to God in our own minds and hearts. Think about a time that you might need extra courage from God, and ask God to be with you then. (Allow three minutes for this quiet prayer.)

LEADER: I would like each of you to come forward now,
one at a time, so that I might bless you.
In the Bible, blessings were often given with oil,
because oil was a sign of strength.
And so I will bless you with oil.

(Call each child forward by name. As you make
the sign of the cross on each forehead with the
oil, say this blessing: "——————, may God
help you to be brave so you can make good
choices." After each blessing, the total group
should respond "Amen.")

LEADER: Now that we have been signed with the oil of
strength, let us pray together to God in the words
that Jesus taught us. Notice that in this prayer we
ask God to "lead us not into temptation."
This is another way of saying: Help us to be
brave enough to make wise choices. Let us now
pray...

ALL: Our Father, who art in heaven,
hallowed be thy name.
Thy kingdom come,
thy will be done,
on earth as it is in heaven.
Give us this day our daily bread,
and forgive us our trespasses
as we forgive those who
trespass against us.
And lead us not into temptation,
but deliver us from evil.
Amen.

Sharing the Good News

BE HAPPY, IT'S EASTER!

Note: In our culture, Easter is not a celebrated season. After Easter Sunday, little is made of this 50-day period that culminates on Pentecost Sunday. Before praying this service (which should be done shortly after Easter Sunday), talk to children about the importance of remembering Jesus and his resurrection, not just on Easter Sunday, but all through the Easter season, and indeed, all through the year.

To Prepare: Place on your prayer table a Bible (open to Mark 16:16), paper and pencils for each participant, and a poster with these words printed on it: "Share the Good News!"

LEADER: On Easter Sunday we all heard the words: "Alleluia, Alleluia!" Does anyone know what they mean?

(Allow time for answers or comments.)

Some of you thought alleluia means "Hurray" and that's very close. The exact meaning is "Praise God," but we use the word "Alleluia" because it sounds so happy and excited.

Easter Sunday is over, but, guess what? When you go to church for the next few weeks you will still hear the words "Alleluia, Alleluia!" This is because Christians are so happy about the resurrection of Jesus that they want to keep on remembering and celebrating it.

One of the ways we can keep celebrating Easter is to tell other people about it. We can spread the good news that Jesus is risen from the dead and is still with us in spirit. This is what Jesus asked his followers to do when he spoke to them after the resurrection. Let's listen to what he said.

READER: A reading from the Gospel of Mark:

After he had risen from the dead,
Jesus showed himself to his followers while they
were at supper.
First he scolded them
for not believing that he was alive.
And then he said to them:
"Go out to the whole world;
spread the good news that I am alive
to all creation."
    After he had spoken to them,
the Lord Jesus was taken up to heaven; there at
the right hand of God
he took his place.
His followers, doing as he asked,
went out and spread the good news."

This is the Word of the Lord.

ALL: Thanks be to God.

LEADER: We, too, are followers of Jesus, and so, we, too, should be spreading the Good News that Jesus is alive. One way we can do this is by remembering it ourselves. We can think about the fact that Jesus is still with us and we can talk to Jesus in our hearts.

Another way is to show by our words and actions that we are followers of the risen Jesus.

A third way is to write about the good news in a letter to someone, and today that's what we are going to do. As you do this, remember the words of Jesus: "Spread the good news that I am alive to the whole world."

(Distribute the paper and pencils. Older children can choose to whom they wish to write an Easter message and address their letters accordingly. Younger children might simply write a message to take home, for example: "Be happy, Jesus is risen." Encourage them to deliver their messages either by mail or in person.)

LEADER: Let us now join hands as we pray:
Jesus, we want to share the news that you are alive and among us through your Holy Spirit. Teach us how to show others that we believe in you. We're very happy that you are with us. Alleluia, Alleluia. Amen.

ALL: Alleluia, Alleluia. Amen.

Knowing We're Not Alone
THE HOLY SPIRIT IS WITH US

Note: This service emphasizes the presence of Jesus through his Holy Spirit. It can be used on or near Pentecost, but is also appropriate for year-round use. Children studying the sacraments, particularly confirmation, might benefit from this emphasis on the gift of the Holy Spirit.

To Prepare: Beforehand, make small verse cards for each child on which is printed the words: "Come, Holy Spirit." Place on the prayer table a Bible (open to John 14:23-27), and a candle.

LEADER: The grace of our Lord Jesus Christ, the love of God, and the fellowship of the Holy Spirit be with you all.

ALL: And also with you.

LEADER: We have heard this greeting often, but perhaps have never thought much about it. It was written by Saint Paul in one of his letters to the people of Corinth. What a wonderful blessing! Wouldn't it be great if we could have the grace of Jesus, the love of God, and the fellowship of the Holy Spirit? But what are these gifts?

(Ask children to reflect aloud about grace, love, and the fellowship of the Holy Spirit. Explain that grace is a spiritual gift; through it we share in God's own life, as God's children. Love is more easily understood. However, you might want to explain that *true* love is "unselfish." By the "fellowship" of the Holy Spirit is meant that God's own Spirit is always with us, as companion and friend.)

LEADER: On the night before he died, Jesus promised his followers that he would give these gifts,

especially the gift of the Holy Spirit. Listen to
the words he used:

READER: A reading from the Gospel of John:

If you love me, Jesus said,
you will keep my word,
and my Father will love you,
and we shall come to you
and make our home with you.
Those who do not love me
do not keep my word...
I have said these things to you
while I am still with you,
but the Holy Spirit,
the one whom the Father will send
to you in my name,
will teach you everything
and remind you of all that I have said.

This is the Word of the Lord.

ALL: Thanks be to God.

LEADER: Let us now ask the Holy Spirit to be with us in a special way and to remind us of all that Jesus has taught us. Please respond, "Come, Holy Spirit."

•You are our companion and friend...

ALL: Come, Holy Spirit.

•You are our teacher and helper...

ALL: Come, Holy Spirit.

•You are our protector and guide...

ALL: Come, Holy Spirit.

LEADER: Jesus has offered us the gift of the Holy Spirit. It is through the presence of the Spirit that Jesus is with us. Often throughout the day we can pray by saying, "Come, Holy Spirit." To remind you of this prayer, I invite each of you to come forward now.

(Call each child by name and present each with a verse card while saying: "_____, receive this card and remember that the Spirit of Jesus is always with you." Invite the children to decorate their cards, either in class or at home, and to place them in their rooms as a prayer reminder.)

Leaving for the Summer
A FAREWELL BLESSING

Note: This service should be one of the last activities you do during your final class of the year. It can be done in your class or meeting room, but it might also be done in church.

To Prepare: In your prayer space, place a Bible (open to John 14: 15-17), a candle, and a large poster, on which is printed these words: "I am with you always." Have available yellow cut-out circles (2" x 2"), and crayons or markers for each child.

LEADER: Blessed are you, Lord God of all creation.

ALL: Blessed be your name forever.

LEADER: Blessed are you, Jesus, Son of God. You are with us now through your Holy Spirit, and you will be with us all through the days of summer. Give us your gifts of faith, hope, love, and knowledge that we might remember your presence and speak to you often. You have promised to be with us and we are reminded of this promise in the Bible.

(Invite children to listen now to God's Word.)

READER: A reading from the Gospel of John:

Jesus said to his friends,
"If you love me, you will keep
the commandments I have given you
and I shall ask the Father to give you
someone to stand by you,
to be with you always.
I am talking about the Spirit of truth....
This Spirit is with you now
and will remain in your hearts.
I am not going to leave you

alone in the world;
I am coming to you again.
This is the Word of the Lord.

ALL: Thanks be to God.

LEADER: Let us now pray to God quietly in our hearts. Let us especially ask for the gift of remembrance— to remember that Jesus is always with us.

(Allow two minutes for this.)

LEADER: As a sign of our desire to remember that Jesus is with us, I invite each of you to write your name on one of these sun-shaped circles.

(Distribute the circles.)

When you finish, please come forward to attach your circle to this poster.

(Hold up the poster for all to see. When all the circles have been attached, continue as follows:)

When you come to Mass this summer, look for this poster and let it remind you that Jesus is with you. Now, before you leave, I want to offer all of you a summer blessing. Please stand.

(If several classes or groups are participating, leaders might say the blessing in unison—with hands extended over the children.)

LEADER: Go now, children, and know that the Spirit of Jesus will be watching over you. Go now and enjoy God's summer gifts of warm sun, cooling waters, and long, light evenings.

Go now, children, with the gift of faith,
that you might see God's hand
in all your work and play.
Go now with the gift of hope,
that you might know God's guidance,
which is keeping you safe.
Go now with the gift of love,
that you might offer love and care
to all you meet.
Go now with the gift of knowledge,
remembering all that you have learned.
With God's help, live it.
Go now, children,
with these words of Jesus in your hearts:
"I will not leave you alone;
I am with you always."

(If possible, hang the poster in the vestibule of
the church so the children can see it during the
summer.)

APPENDIX

The following prayers appear in these services. You might want to
practice them and/or have children memorize them before
you pray the services in which they appear.

May the peace of Christ be with you.
Response: And also with you.

The grace of our Lord, Jesus Christ, the love of God,
and the fellowship of the Holy Spirit be with you all.
Response: And also with you.

This is the Word of the Lord.
Response: Thanks be to God.

Hail Mary, full of grace, the Lord is with you. Blessed are you among
women, and blessed is the fruit of your womb, Jesus.
Holy Mary, mother of God, pray for us sinners, now and at the hour
of our death. Amen.

Holy, holy, holy, Lord God of hosts. Heaven and earth are full
of your glory. Blessed is he who comes in the name of the Lord.
Response: Hosanna in the highest.

Lord, have mercy.
Christ, have mercy.
Lord, have mercy.

Blessed are you, Lord, God of all creation. Through your

goodness we have bread to offer, which earth has given
and human hands have made. It will become for us
the bread of life.
Response: Blessed be God forever.

_____

Blessed are you, Lord, God of all creation. Through your goodness we
have wine to offer, fruit of the vine and work of human hands.
It will become our spiritual drink.
Response: Blessed be God forever.

_____

Glory be to the Father, and to the Son, and to the Holy Spirit, as it was
in the beginning, is now, and ever shall be, world without end. Amen.

_____

In the name of the Father, and of the Son, and of the Holy Spirit.
Amen.

_____

Our Father, who art in heaven, hallowed be thy name. Thy kingdom
come, thy will be done, on earth as it is in heaven. Give us this day
our daily bread, and forgive us our trespasses as we forgive those
who trespass against us. And lead us not into temptation, but deliver
us from evil. Amen.

_____

The following prayer refrains are also used in these services:

Glory and praise to you, Lord Jesus Christ.

Lord, hear our prayer.

Amen. So be it. Amen.

We give you thanks.

Come, Lord Jesus, come.

Come, Holy Spirit.

Alleluia, Alleluia.

Thanks be to God.

All praise and honor to you, Lord Jesus Christ.

Blessed are you forever.

We praise and thank you, God.

Thank you, God, for pets.

Jesus was born on Christmas Day. All of us can celebrate!
All of us can rejoice!

THEME INDEX

Nature and the Four Seasons

Special Themes

Also by Gwen Costello

Prayer Services for Religious Educators
Christians who share their faith with others through religious instruction now
have a unique resource both for various occasions and for specific needs of catechists, parents, lay ministers, parish leaders, children, and teenagers/young
adults. The services offer complete prayer experiences in a brief, accessible style.

Paper, 8 1/2 x 11, 80 pp., $9.95

Stations of the Cross for Teenagers
These 14 "personalized" reflections on the journey of Jesus toward Calvary are
clear and simple, relating directly to the real life situations of today's teens. Concerns address dealing with peers and parents, success at school and in the eyes of
friends, accepting failure, suicide and death, drugs, and relationship of faith to
life.

Paper, illustrated, $1.95

A Bible Way of the Cross for Children
Upper primary and intermediate grade children will respond positively as each
station begins with an appropriate Scripture passage, then meditation, prayer,
and actions.

Paper, illustrated, $1.95

Lenny Learns about Lent
Children here learn of the significance of Ash Wednesday, the prayer practice of
the Stations of the Cross, and the three great celebrations of the Triduum.

VHS, $29.95

Holydays and Holidays *(with Richard Costello)*
Prepare yourselves and your children for adventurous journeys to mark and celebrate the various holydays and holidays throughout the school year.

Each of 8 videos purchased separately, $29.95;
all 8 videos, including guides, $209.65.

Following Jesus Through the Church Year *(with Richard Costello)*
Delightful cartoon character, Krispin, enables primary grade children to explore
the meaning of Advent, Christmas, Lent, Easter, and Pentecost.

Each of the 8 videos purchased separately, $29.95;
all 8 videos, including guides, $209.65.